THE WASHINGTON PAPERS

5: Neo-Isolationism and the World of the Seventies

Walter Laqueur

THE CENTER FOR STRATEGIC AND INTERNATIONAL STUDIES
Georgetown University, Washington, D.C.

THE LIBRARY PRESS
New York

1972

5: Neo-Isolationism and the World of the Seventies

5: Neo-Isolationism and the World of the Seventies

This Washington Paper is a much enlarged and rewritten version of an essay originally published in two installments in *Commentary* (August and September 1972). I am grateful for the permission given by the editor of *Commentary*, published by the American Jewish Committee, to reproduce the sections of this paper which originally appeared in its pages.

PART ONE

Permissive society has encouraged outspokenness in the discussion of sexual matters in life and literature, but in political debate Victorian standards prevail; euphemism and circumlocution are more frequent than they were a decade or two ago. Thus a great many synonyms for retreat have been added to the American political dictionary in recent years. It is only rarely that someone with refreshing candor and without undue inhibitions states that "the decade of the sixties has produced a new school of isolationism," adding that "they [the young Americans] see no country for whose security they would fight."[1]

The facts are hardly in dispute. And yet, to advocate isolationism openly is no more fashionable than to shout for more Vietnams. "Isolationism has been dead for a quarter of a century," says Ronald Steel, "the country—and particularly younger Americans who are eager to help the underprivileged peoples of the Third World—is not going to turn its back on other nations."[2] Such assertions, needless to say, have to be taken with a grain of salt: are young Americans really all that eager to help the underprivileged peoples of the Third World? "The public figures associated with the movement—people like Fulbright, Kennedy and Galbraith—are hardly prewar provincials," says David Calleo, as if anyone had ever claimed that they were. Another writer suggests that we should take the chimera "new isolationism" and "throw it away, as far as possible."[3] The neo-isolationists, in short, are very sensitive; they are also a little unjust toward the prewar isolationists, many of whom, incidentally, also rejected the label of isolationism.

In a study published several years ago, Professor Manfred Jonas recalled some useful facts about the chief advocates of isolationism in the thirties. Senator Nye was heir to the traditions of the Nonpartisan League and of agrarian radicalism; Senator Borah led the fight for the Kellog-Briand pact in 1928; John Bassett Moore spent a lifetime trying to strengthen and expand the scope of international law. Norman Thomas, Oswald Garrison Villard and Charles Beard were neither backwoodsmen nor reactionaries; the list of causes they supported was a more or less complete catalog of American reform movements of the twentieth century.[4] The isolationists, or at any rate most of their leading spokesmen, did not oppose world trade; they were not heartless creatures but believed, as did Senator Borah, that America could never be indifferent should suffering visit any part of the human race. Many sympathized with the Allies in their struggle against Hitler.

There are, of course, basic differences between the isolationism of the thirties and the mood today, if only because technology and modern arms systems have made a total retreat from world politics quite impossible. But the basic inspiration is often the same, and so, too, are the slogans: If Senator Fulbright invokes John Quincy Adams ("to be the well wishers to the freedom and independence of all, the champion and vindicator only of her own"), this is precisely the quotation that always figured in the writings of the thirties. It is taken from the Washington Address of 1821 and appears also as Mr. Steel's motto in his *Pax Americana.* Granted that Fulbright and most other spokesmen of non-interventionism do not advocate "a wholesale renunciation by the United States of its global responsibilities," but merely want to "redress the heavy imbalance on the side of foreign commitment." They simply want to turn away from "obsessive and indiscriminate globalism."

It is not readily obvious what advice John Quincy Adams is able to offer in the present world situation. It is no doubt reassuring to know that America will "recommend the general cause of liberty by the countenance of her voice, and by the benignant sympathy of her example." But just as the countenance of my voice alone would not be sufficient to give great comfort to Senator Fulbright if he were to be attacked by muggers on a Washington street, it is difficult to see what help America's benign example would bring to nations under attack. Senator Fulbright has spoken and written eloquently about the American hubris, the *vertige de puissance;* he is less modest when it comes to claims for American superiority on the moral plane: "America is the only nation equipped to lead the world in an effort to change the nature of its politics." This is a formidable claim and I doubt whether it can be substantiated. There is more genuine participatory democracy in Luxembourg, in Holland, or in most Swiss cantons than there is or will be in the United States for the predictable future. Schwyz and Unterwalden could make a far stronger case for moral leadership in the world, but one somehow doubts whether the Russians would be impressed.

The more thoughtful advocates of non-interventionism are aware that the policy they espouse involves certain difficulties. Mr. Steel, for instance, realizes that it would not only have precluded Santo Domingo, but also United States intervention against Franco during the Spanish Civil War.[5] This is of course a bitter pill to swallow, and the non-interventionists try to sweeten it with reasoning which is scarcely convincing. Mr. Steel argues that although the outcome of the Spanish Civil War was tragic, "it is far from clear that it would have been less tragic had we intervened. If self-determination, which we continually trumpet as our guiding principle, means anything, it means the right of nations to work out their own internal arrangements, however painful that might be." But this is shirking the real issue, which was not, as was immediately pointed out to Mr. Steel, letting Spain work out its internal arrangements, but counteracting Hitler's and Mussolini's intervention.

The case for opting out of world politics is seldom pursued to its logical, radical conclusion; far more frequent are the half-hearted arguments, the compromises, the suggestions of "discriminate interventionism," of "partial disengagement," of "measured disinvolvement." Again, a fairly strong case could be made if it were admitted that the burden has become too heavy for America, and that other countries have not been willing to share it. Instead, to fortify their case, the advocates of neo-isolationism have been trying to show that their policy is not just a necessary evil, but desirable from every aspect because it corresponds to changes that have taken place all over the globe with the end of the cold war. They play down Soviet strength and maintain that if there is still any danger from those parts—which is not certain—it is exclusively political.

There is a certain consistency to such arguments, for if it can be shown that the Russian danger is largely mythical, the case against globalism is irrefutable. A few examples should suffice: Fulbright believes that both Khrushchev and his successors have been sincere in their stated belief that ideological warfare would be conducted by peaceful economic competition. A reconciliation between West and East is, according to Senator Fulbright, primarily a psychological problem; the building of economic and cultural bridges could pave the way for the reunification of Europe, for as it becomes clear to each side that it is safe and profitable to do business with the other, ideological barriers could be expected to crumble.[6]

Similar opinions, albeit phrased a little more cautiously, have been expressed in the writings of other experts on international affairs. According to Messrs. Stillman and Pfaff, "there has been a catastrophic decline of Soviet foreign influence and prestige;" they assume that a German settlement on reasonable terms will be followed within a few years by the disintegration of whatever authority the Soviets retain in the region. Or, as Fulbright puts it, "the foundations of the East German puppet state would be expected to erode." Mr. Steel has reached the conclusion that the "Communist world does not exist any more." More cautiously, Professor Hans Morgenthau maintains that the Communist world is being transformed into a pluralistic universe. According to one recent account, the young generation in America believes that the Soviet Union is an "established, status quo oriented power;" it considers current Soviet declarations about the aims of Soviet policy "relics of the past" and feels that liberalization has taken place in Eastern Europe. On this specific subject it is in agreement with David Calleo, according to whom Russia's intervention in Czechoslovakia was carried out "with considerable hesitation and constraint."[7]

It is admittedly unfair to single out any particular author or statement in this enormous literature; I have not chosen the most extreme among them but picked a few which seem typical. These predictions of yesteryear have so far not been borne out by events. There has been no catastrophic decline in Soviet foreign influence and prestige; East Germany is going as strong as ever, and there is no good reason to assume that it will disappear. There has been no liberalization in Eastern Europe; the Soviet Union has not become a status quo power and the Communist "pluralistic universe" is largely mythical. On the contrary, the Soviet Union has reestablished its authority over most Communist parties in the world—even Yugoslavia and Romania have again drawn closer to Moscow. Russia has been quite successful in containing China. There has been a setback in Egypt but it is too early to tell if it was a lasting one: when the dust has settled in Cairo, it may well be that the Russians are still there but that Sadat is not. In any event, the Soviet Union now has a base in Iraq and, all things considered, the Persian Gulf is more important than the Sinai desert. True, I. F. Stone (*New York Review,* 29 June 1972) has reached the conclusion that President Nixon has softened up the Russians with special favors and persuaded them to become America's junior partner. But it is unlikely, to put it mildly, that he will find many converts to his thesis in Europe or the Middle East, in South East Asia or the Far East, anywhere, in effect, outside Washington and New York. On a more serious level, Mr. Kennan has recently announced that "world revolution has simply faded out of the picture as a concrete aim of Soviet foreign policy;" but for the dangerous nuclear and naval rivalry, the outside world and particularly the United States would have little more to fear from Russia than it did in 1910. There is no reason to consider her a serious threat to American security.[8] Soviet leaders are insecure at home, Mr. Kennan maintains, because they are dimly conscious, as was the Tsarist regime seventy years ago, that they have lost the confidence of their own intellectuals and don't know how to recover it.

Whether Soviet intellectuals today put more or less confidence in their leaders than they did fifteen or thirty years ago is a moot point. But what does it matter? *Oderint dum metuant.* Mr. Kennan, at Princeton, seems to ignore the fact that the impact of disaffected intelligentsia on politics is not quite the same in the Soviet Union as in his own country. That world revolution was no longer a concrete aim of Soviet foreign policy should have been clear to Mr. X back in 1947 when he wrote his famous article for *Foreign Affairs.* American security was certainly not threatened at that time; the issue at stake was the struggle for Europe, and Mr. Kennan now seems to believe, for no good reason, that it has ended.

There is, of course, a certain continuity in the foreign policy of every nation, but that does not mean that the Soviet regime is as weak as the Tsarist government facing imminent doom or that it no longer wants to expand its sphere of influence. Mr. Kennan assumes that revolutionary regimes are expansionist and that postrevolutionary ones are not. Napoleon, for one, was not aware of this fact. The Soviet Union may ultimately become a status quo power, but American neo-isolationism will hardly hasten this process. On the contrary, it will create opportunities for the expansion of Soviet influence which did not exist in the past, and which the Russians would be foolish not to exploit.

* * * * *

Those who question whether isolationism is a practical proposition in the near future voice the most radical version of the neo-isolationist argument, for they believe that while the Vietnam war was certainly a mistake, it was not an accident; American interventionism is a reflection of American society and America's imperialist wars will cease only if that society is changed. According to the same authorities, big business is running American foreign policy: the economic prosperity of the United States increasingly depends on overseas expansion. America, in brief, has to be interventionist for economic reasons.

This thesis has the advantage of simplicity and consistency, but is it borne out by the facts? How to explain that in World War I, for apparently no good reason, America supported its economic rivals against Germany, with which it had no economic conflict, and that in the Second World War it made the same mistake? The revisionists claim that in the thirties "Roosevelt cast his lot with the nations that were least inimical to the interest of the American establishment" (Sidney Lens). But there was not the slightest economic friction between the Berlin-Rome axis and the American establishment, whereas Britain was a major rival and the Soviet Union not exactly its idol.

It could, of course, be argued that out of shortsightedness or stupidity big business has not always acted according to its best interests. But, if it acts so consistently against its interests, the revisionist theories become a little suspect. How does one explain American support for Israel despite the fact that economic interests in the Middle East militate against such a policy? And to explain the Vietnam war in economic terms is no more plausible. American imports from the whole of Indochina were $11 million in 1950; why spend more than a thousand times that sum to dominate a country in which there were virtually no American investments? Capitalist business is not run on these lines.

And so Mr. Sidney Lens, author of a huge volume on American imperialism which betrays more passion than familiarity with the subject, reluctantly reaches the conclusion that "tin and tungsten could not justify the enormous commitment Johnson was making." Others, failing to identify the particular economic interests that allegedly shaped American foreign policy, have asserted that the future of the whole system was at stake.

This is admittedly the extremist thesis; not all revisionists claim that American foreign and defense policy is run by big business. Mr. Steel notes, quite correctly: "We have not exploited our empire; our empire has exploited us." Professor Melman has noted that the Department of Defense is by no means run by big business, but that, on the contrary, the Department of Defense bureaucracy frequently makes decisions which directly and profoundly affect the economy.

In the final analysis even the extremists cannot quite make up their minds between the Leninist fundamentalist thesis, which they say greatly impresses them, and psychological explanations. But then Lenin, too, would have found it difficult to make sense of certain strange phenomena in the contemporary world—the spectacle of leading businessmen falling over each other in their eagerness to make deals with Russia and China, for instance. Their class interest apparently has ceased to function, or do they perhaps believe (in contrast to Mr. Lens) that the future of the capitalist system is no longer at stake?

The basic tenets of this school of thought can be summarized under the following headings:

1. America needs the underdeveloped countries for its investments and as a market for exports.
2. It needs them as suppliers of raw materials.
3. Economic prosperity in the United States thus depends on exploiting the Third World.
4. Big business has much to gain from the continuing national security crisis.
5. Therefore only radical structural change—a revolution— in American society will make American foreign policy non-imperialist and thus peaceful.

The first point, once the crux of the Leninist argument, is no longer seriously maintained except by a few fundamentalists. Neither facts nor figures will bear it out. The second thesis, on the other hand, still has a great many believers. They admit that American business is not anxious to invest in the Third World and that more and more of its trade is with the developed countries. But, according to the Magdoff-Kolko school, America needs columbium and beryllium and titanium and certain other rare metals, crucial components for its heavy industry. Is it not then true that American living standards depend on those minerals and that consequently America must be imperialist and cannot withdraw into its national boundaries? With even greater justice it could be demonstrated that Sweden has to pursue an imperialist policy; there is no industrial nation which has all or even most of these rare metals. All of them have to import these materials from various far away places—not, incidentally, including Vietnam, Laos, or Cambodia. Since there are no absolutely autarkic national economies in this world, with the possible exception of some of the most primitive agrarian societies, the outlook is unpromising.

Every industrialized society has to be imperialist, and the smaller it is, the more aggressive it has to be to get the raw materials it needs. This, of course, is manifestly absurd, quite apart from the fact that the dependence of the industrially developed countries on the Third World for raw materials has steadily declined over the last few decades as synthetic materials replace raw materials. Oil is the exception that proves the rule, for whatever one's views about Colonel Qadafi, he certainly has not behaved like an imperialist stooge. The economic prosperity of the United States and the other leading industrial countries does not depend on the Third World; if it did, one could be more optimistic about the future of the underdeveloped countries.

Nor is it true that big business has a vested interest in the armaments race. The interests of certain big enterprises are involved but this is not quite the same. It really ought to be common knowledge by now that the greatest economic advances of the fifties and sixties were made by Japan, West Germany, and Italy, the very countries in which defense spending was low, or, as in the case of Japan, virtually nonexistent. German heavy industry has been in a healthier state since it stopped making guns.

We are left with the argument that lasting peace will come only after radical structural changes amounting virtually to a revolution have taken place in the United States. Such changes may or may not be desirable, according to one's political views, but the assumption that they would make for a stable peace is quite untenable in the light of historical experience. China is Communist and so is the Soviet Union, yet the relationship between the two is probably the main source of concern in today's world. Even a Communist America would be a big power, and would certainly assert its influence in world affairs. Since it would not be impeded—as it is today—by strong pacifist trends on the domestic scene and by anti-imperialist guilt feelings, a "restructured America" would probably pursue a more aggressive foreign policy than it does at present.

It is, of course, tedious to go over familiar ground, and to refute the revisionists is not much of an intellectual challenge. Their arguments are manifestly untenable in the light of realities, but it would be overoptimistic to assume that they will be discarded. They are, and probably will remain, articles of faith for many Americans, corresponding as they do to deeply held beliefs in the behind-the-scene activities of sinister forces, in conspiracies and plots. These beliefs are most commonly found on the extreme right and the extreme left of the political spectrum but are by no means confined to them. The genealogy of the conspiracy theory of history leads from the Abbé Barruel, who claimed that the French revolution was the work of the *illuminati;* to the "Protocols of the Elders of Zion;" from the belief, widespread in the nineteen-twenties, that the arms and ammunition producers had caused the First World War; to the assertion that Kuhn, Loeb and Co. had financed Hitler's rise to power; and most recently to the revisionist school of historiography rewriting the history of the cold war.

Such explanations frequently, though not always, have an appearance of verisimilitude; their advocates usually present them with utter conviction—in marked contrast to the conscientious historian who will stress that historical events are usually highly complex, that they cannot be reduced to a single cause or motive, and that accident and contingency always play important roles. That is why the conspiracy theory of history is far more likely to become a political force; political movements cannot be based on "perhaps" or "maybe," on complex and inconclusive analyses when clear and unambiguous answers are needed to sustain the faith of believers. And there will always be historians, sociologists, and economists willing to squeeze the facts a little, to select those likely to fortify their political arguments and to ignore the others which do not fit their preconceived schemes.

* * * * *

It is only a dozen years since President Kennedy in his inaugural address declared: "Let every nation know, whether it wishes us well or ill, that we shall pay any price, bear any burden, meet any hardship, support any friend, oppose any foe, to assure the survival and success of liberty." Since then the pendulum has swung to the other extreme and the reasons for this swing will be studied for a long time to come. Was the source of the evil the Truman Doctrine, as some claim, or the decision to apply the Truman Doctrine outside Europe and the Near East? Vietnam no doubt precipitated the process and exacerbated the crisis. But is it not likely that the process of "disinvolvement" would sooner or later have come to pass anyway, albeit less suddenly and less radically?

The United States was drawn into a leading role in world politics as a result of the Second World War which destroyed the old equilibrium in Europe. It did so without much enthusiasm, without real experience, and without strong support from public opinion. The anti-Communist hysteria of the early fifties was hardly a firm basis on which to build a global policy. There was no long-range perspective; the measures taken were on an *ad hoc* basis in response to the actions of the other side. Yet as a result America became involved—politically, financially and militarily— in many parts of the globe, and this overinvolvement, it is now argued, put too great a strain on her power: America failed to distinguish between what was desirable and essential (Morgenthau); it fell victim to the "illusion of American omnipotence" (Brogan); its foreign policy became unlimited in geographical scope. It wanted to instill order into an inherently disorderly world. Public opinion became more and more restive; was it not a fact that instead of being a liberating force America had become a glorified prison warden? What had globalism to show on the credit side a quarter of a century after the end of the Second World War—many billions of dollars spent for purposes that were not visibly in the national interest, and an involvement in seemingly permanent conflict, including a nasty war in a distant country supporting regimes that were not exemplars of liberty and democracy.

This war cost tens of thousands of American lives, not to

mention the immense financial burden. It devastated wide stretches of Vietnam, it brought in its wake all the brutalities of modern warfare, and it was clear by 1967 at the latest that it would not end in victory. In the circumstances, it was not surprising that opposition grew, opposition not just to Vietnam but to the whole policy and the assumptions underlying it, which had landed America in the Vietnam morass. The burden had clearly become intolerable and a powerful reaction set in.

So far the historian of the future will have no particular difficulty in understanding how the swing to isolationism set in and how it gathered momentum. But he will still be baffled by some crucial questions which, at a distance of several decades, may well appear inexplicable. I do not mean the excesses of the isolationist reaction, the built-in exaggerations, the inclination to throw the baby out with the bath water. Overreaction is not unprecedented in the annals of history. What will puzzle him much more is that whereas the two superpowers were roughly similar in population at the time, the United States being the much richer and more developed country and certainly not inferior militarily, a foreign policy of "unlimited geographical scope" did not become a burden too heavy to bear for the Soviet Union.

Why did so many Americans rebel against the fact that their country had acquired superpower status, whereas most Russians regarded it as a matter for satisfaction and pride? Perhaps the future historian will explain this curious contrast with reference to the different historical traditions of the two countries; perhaps he will point to mistakes committed by American leaders and the superior tactical ability of the Russians. Very likely he will draw the conclusion, rightly or wrongly, that an American-style democracy was, in the long run, simply incapable of sustaining an active global policy; it lacked the sense of mission, the perseverance and the ruthlessness that globalism demanded.

Many, perhaps most, Americans believed that the State Department, the Pentagon, the CIA, should be run *grosso modo* —like a town meeting in eighteenth century New England; there should be no secrets from friend or foe, and those in charge of the nation's defense and foreign policy should tell the truth, the whole truth and nothing but the truth regardless of circumstances and consequences. If the other side did not abide by the same standards, that was no reason why America should stoop to its reprehensible behavior.

The moral standards prescribed by the critics are exceedingly high—they are also quite frequently disingenuous. For if the private life of these enemies of secrecy and mendacity in public life were judged according to the standards they apply, and if the punishment they wanted to visit on their enemies were to be meted out to them, they would have to spend most of their lives in prison—with the exception perhaps of a few saints. The foreign and defense policies of a big country certainly cannot be run according to these precepts. The only thing that can be said in mitigation is that they may be connected with the fact that, unlike most other countries, America has had the good fortune of never having been invaded or occupied, that it has never faced a real danger, and that it has developed in splendid isolation.

World politics in the sixties and early seventies consisted not only of the American-Soviet confrontation; it was more than a story of American sins of commission and omission. The failure of Europe, once it had rebuilt its economy, to reassert its political strength and military power will appear even more inexplicable to the future historian. How could the Europeans fail to understand that above all it was their own fate that was at stake? How could they not realize that sooner or later Americans would lose patience with a continent that failed to pull its weight in accordance with its potential and its resources?

It is true that the forces of inertia and of active opposition in Europe were strong; yet more important was paralysis of will, for there was no conscious abdication among the Europeans. Instead, lethargy and parochial interests proved stronger than unifying forces; and they were reinforced by the unthinking belief that somehow or other the security and independence of the Continent would be assured and that for a long time to come economic cooperation was all that was needed. To shortsightedness and impotence was frequently added a deep conviction in the superior political wisdom of the Europeans compared with the inexperienced Americans. There have been many offenders in this respect, but the French have done more than anyone else to sabotage European unity; the know-nothingism of British Labor, after all, did not have the intellectual pretensions of Gaullism.

De Gaulle's visions and gestures found many admirers at the time because they had a certain grandeur and style. But they were utterly divorced from the realities of world affairs, being based on a ridiculously mistaken analysis of the balance of power, and staking claims for France which were little short of megalomania. Yet Gaullism corresponded to certain deeply held beliefs and emotions in France. Its inheritors, in a style more reminiscent of small shopkeepers than of Don Quixote, still make their collaboration with the other European countries conditional on the fulfillment both of their specific economic demands, however one-sided and unreasonable, and on the assumption that France will play the leading political role in Europe—with Germany as Europe's industrialist and Britain as its banker. The behavior of many European statesmen was such as to sorely try even the patience of saints, and the Americans, needless to say, were no saints.

* * * * *

America in 1972 faces the choice between a policy favoring a "more mature partnership," meaning a more or less orderly retreat from certain global positions which have become untenable, and one demanding a "reordering of priorities," pressing for a much more radical reorientation. The more moderate neo-isolationists suggest a "cool assessment of national interest" as against the "heady intoxication with moral obligations, the penchant for grandiose principles" (R. Steel). But it is not readily obvious why a retreat from moral obligations should stop with national interest. There is nothing sacred about the national interest: with equal justice a case could be made for putting one's class or ethnic group or family or one's own personal affairs above it.

If Mr. Steel argues that the world may be full of wickedness and inequity, but that it has always been so and can therefore get by without American help if necessary, the same case can be made, after all, against progressive income tax and social legislation. Why renounce "idealism" and social obligations in international affairs and stick to them in domestic politics? The poor, after all, are always with us, and a "cool reassessment" of priorities on the domestic scene may well show that since there is not enough money for all anyway there is no good reason to engage in redistributing wealth.

The radical isolationsists have a stronger case than more moderate spokesmen of the movement, for a certain logic cannot be denied to their argument. Why adopt half measures, readers of Professor Tucker's *A New Isolationism* are bound to ask. This study offers the most closely reasoned case for isolationism;[9] through it is not, as some have claimed, a "radical challenge to current orthodoxy of American foreign policy." On the contrary, it expresses in more ways than one the views of the new counterorthodoxy. Mr. Tucker argues that alliances cannot enhance American security; on the contrary, all of them have become liabilities. Even if the Soviet Union were to be in full control of Western Europe, it would not, he maintains, pose a markedly greater threat to America's physical security than it does today. Even placing Soviet missiles in Cuba would not pose a greater menace than the one already held out by Soviet polaris-type submarines. Economically, the United States is remarkably self-sufficient; a policy of autarky would be a viable, though somewhat costly, alternative. America has substantial interests abroad, but these would not necessarily be jeopardized by a military withdrawal. The danger of nuclear proliferation exists, but even if Japan and West Germany had nuclear arms, they would still be constrained to behave moderately because they are so vulnerable. The same applies, *a fortiori,* to smaller countries.

In contrast to most other isolationists, Professor Tucker has few illusions about the consequences of an American retreat; he does not deny that American influence would be substantially reduced with a resultant increase of Soviet influence in Western Europe and other parts of the world. He rejects as naive the assumption that, following a retreat from global politics, America would obtain a strong position of moral leadership or that such a retreat would necessarily result in a striking improvement in the quality of domestic life.

While Mr. Tucker's realism is refreshing after the massive doses of wishful thinking contained in the writings of most other isolationists, there is a striking disparity between his radical analysis and his moderate conclusions. Why propose (as he does) only a relatively small reduction in the defense burden as far as America is concerned? Why not take radical action? If, as he says, there is no danger that the American retreat will result in the Finlandization of Europe, surely there is no reason to assume that either the Russians or the Chinese will invade America.

If the American empire ought to be dismantled, the imperial bureaucracy and the industrial superstructure of the warfare state destroyed before it destroys the nation (as Mr. Steel claims), why not make a truly revolutionary decision? Would not the Russians and the Chinese find it exceedingly difficult to justify the continued existence of their defense establishments once America had opted for total (or near-total) disarmament? If a Soviet presence in Cuba would not really affect the strategic balance, could it not be argued with equal logic that without, say, New Mexico, Arizona and a few other states, the United States would not be markedly worse off than it is today? As for the rest of the United States, would not many of its present problems be more tractable if it were split up into half a dozen sovereign states? And if Europe (or America at that), following some disaster should disappear altogether, this would not mean the extinction of the human race on earth, which as we are reminded with increasing frequency is overpopulated anyway and whose resources are rapidly dwindling.

Once one engages in playing the game of "thinking the unthinkable" (Senator Church on Tucker's book) there is no room for arbitrarily drawing a line. Mr. Tucker, needless to say, is absolutely right in assuming that an isolated America is possible, but the crucial question to be asked is at what price? And if the price should be as high as he thinks it likely to be, it is not readily obvious why anyone should advocate paying it.

In the final analysis, Mr. Tucker's views like those of other neo-isolationsists rest, in his own words, "upon a view of the world in which the great powers are increasingly constrained in their behavior, whether towards each other or toward small powers." This may be correct with regard to post-Vietnam America; as far as the rest of the world is concerned it is, at best, a highly optimistic assumption.

Neo-isolationist optimism seems equally unwarranted in other respects. Proliferation and disengagement are two sides of the same coin, writes David Calleo, who believes in a "selective expansion of the nuclear club." The first part of his thesis is beyond dispute, but it is less clear why it should be assumed that the expansion would be selective, and why this policy would result in the existence of a "club" and not in nuclear wars. (Few observers of the Asian scene doubt that India and Pakistan would have used atomic bombs long ago if they had had them.) That neo-isolationism will precipitate nuclear proliferation seems a foregone conclusion which the more thoughtful of the non-interventionists are aware of and have more or less cheerfully accepted.

In the new world order, as they see it, the responsibility for dealing with intractable problems will be transferred to the United Nations. Alternatively, we are referred to the emergence of a "multipolar system" as a cure for contemporary ills, a subject discussed in the first part of this study. And, as a last resort, certain concepts from the past have been disinterred. Ronald Steel (following Walter Lippmann) has praised the advantages of a "mature spheres of interest" policy; David Calleo, evidently preferring more remote history, has referred to the positive lessons to be drawn from the Holy Roman Empire. With equal or greater justice one could point to the Habsburg and Ottoman empires, but unfortunately Senator Fulbright has already preempted them; according to him, these empires failed because they devoted too much time and energy to their foreign policy. A spheres of influence policy has worked during certain periods of history—between Spain and Portugal, between Russia and Britain, and on some other occasions between status quo powers. It could work today if, as Mr. Kennan claims, there were any real similarity between the Soviet Union today and the Russian foreign policy of 1910.

Soviet ambitions, to repeat, are not now, and perhaps never were, unlimited; the ideological impluse in Soviet foreign policy has been steadily diminishing over several decades. This process will in all probability continue in the years to come if further expansion of the Soviet sphere of influence were seen to involve unacceptable risks. By the same token, this trend will be halted or even reversed if American foreign policy turns to neo-isolationism. The more thoughtful neo-isolationists are aware that they face a dilemma: on one hand they freely admit that a *Pax Sovietica* would be a universal disaster (R. Steel); on the other they recommend that Washington shun all military alliances. The obvious, indeed, the *only* way out of this dilemma is to exaggerate the difficulties facing the Soviet leaders on the domestic front and to prove that any attempt on their part to expand their sphere of influence is unlikely because it would do them more harm than good. Messrs. Brezhnev and Kosygin will be grateful for such solicitous advice, but there is no reason to assume that they will follow it.

The Moscow summit has given birth to a joint declaration affirming twelve common principles as admirable as the United Nations Charter and just as vague; each side will interpret it in a different way. America, the status quo power, assumes that the world scene will remain more or less as it is now for many years to come. The Soviet Union on the other hand assumes that this does not preclude gradually squeezing America out of Europe and the Mediterranean, containing China, and take-overs by pro-Soviet forces in various parts of the world. Based on this reckoning, new conflicts are bound to arise sooner or later. Certain rules of the game have been established, but the Soviet Union has never made it a secret that it intends to change them as the balance of power tilts in its favor. Whether this is going to happen will depend mainly on future American administrations.

No doubt the prospects appear favorable to the Russians. To again quote Mr. Steel, one American advocate of disinvolvement, "The Vietnam war has triggered off a profound revulsion against involvement in all foreign quarrels .... The American people have been cynically, even cruelly used by political leaders who have squandered their wealth and stolen the lives of their children to fight imperial wars." In this respect, as in many others, there is not the faintest symmetry between the United States and the Soviet Union. Although there may be grumbling in the Soviet Union about squandering good money on Cuba and Egypt (which the Russians can afford even less than the Americans); although a few intellectuals may have pangs of conscience about Czechoslovakia; although there may be other similar complaints; the chances that such a mood will affect any sizeable sections of Soviet society, that, in other words, it will become a political force, are virtually nil.

Neo-isolationism as a mood, an expression of boredom or revulsion with world politics, is psychologically understandable. But the neo-isolationist creed breaks down once its spokesmen attempt to provide a more or less coherent and ideologically respectable justification. There is no reason to assume that neo-isolationism will make for a more peaceful world or that it will solve any problems at all. If neo-isolationism has a claim to moral superiority, it is roughly speaking that of Pontius Pilate. Above all, the basic reasoning underlying the neo-isolationist argument is profoundly mistaken: the assumption that turning one's back on foreign affairs will make it any easier to tackle America's domestic problems—the urban crisis, the unsolved social and racial questions, the alienation of wide sections of American society, pollution physical and mental.

A confident, dynamic country can play an active part in world affairs and at the same time cope with its internal problems. A people adrift, lacking purpose and conviction, will not be able to achieve either; defeatism is a disease that cannot be compartmentalized. Can those really be trusted and relied upon who claim that while they are disgusted with foreign policy they would be only too eager to do their utmost on the home front? If America has neglected its domestic problems, this has not been the result of an excess of idealism, intellectual effort, or emotional involvement in foreign affairs; foreign affairs have always preoccupied only a small minority. It is often argued that "a nation cannot do for others what it cannot do for itself." But such sweeping statements are questionable both on the collective and the individual level. The fact that nations, as individuals, are not perfect does not, and should not, prevent them from aiding others. Sometimes, ironically, they can do for others precisely what they cannot do for themselves.

Would a reallocation of financial resources solve the problem? Economists have noted an apparent paradox: during the last year of World War II more than 35 percent of the American G.N.P. was spent on defense, a proportion about five times as high as at present. Yet the war did not inhibit social change and the average American was not notably worse off than five years before or after. This, needless to say, is not an argument for war as a cure for social ills. But neither does it follow that the domestic effects of "interventionism" are all debilitating. And the assumption that, but for "globalism," the cities would be habitable, poverty would have been stamped out, and the disaffected be reintegrated is an unwarranted one. If confidence and optimism have been lost, they will not be restored by dollar transfusions, nor will they be found in the backwoods far from the evils of the defense establishment and foreign policy. To paraphrase Peter Wiles: the only certain result of a Greening-of-America policy would be the emergence of Russia as the dominant power in Europe and perhaps other parts of the globe. The rest is wishful thinking.

Neo-isolationism is a mansion with many rooms; its advocates range from the sensible to the lunatic fringe. Generalizations on this subject, like all generalizations, are bound to do injustice to some of them. A critique of neo-isolationism cannot ignore the grave mistakes that gave rise to the present crisis, which in its turn has produced the climate in which isolationism has flourished. It has to accept the limitations of American power and it does not propagate "indiscriminate globalism." It does not claim that positions which have become untenable should be maintained. It does want to do away with prevailing illusions about the consequences of "decommitment." If neo-isolationism should become official American policy the results would be more or less predictable. However frightening the short-term results of such policy might be, in the long run, admittedly, there is little cause for alarm, for the realities of world politics have a wonderfully sobering effect in restoring the mental balance of those who have lost their bearings. Roosevelt, in 1939, could not convince

Senator Vandenberg but the Japanese at Pearl Harbor did. One may hope that the price America and the world are bound to pay for the political education of the neo-isolationists will not be too heavy, nor the damage irreparable.

PART TWO

To summarize: It is not difficult to understand neo-isolationism as a mood. Americans have paid a high price for "globalism" and there have been few rewards. The ideological underpinnings of neo-isolationism have been outlined with increasing frequency; it has been explained not just as a mood but as the logical, inevitable answer to a new world situation. It has been argued that there is a great deal of symmetry between the positions of the two superpowers; both the United States and the Soviet Union are in the declining days of their condominium and both have grudgingly accepted this state of affairs. New centers of power are rapidly emerging in various parts of the world. They provide a genuine regional balance of power and thus the preconditions for a real détente. The two superpowers have drawn nearer, they are turning away from their obsolete global ambitions and their increasingly lunatic arms race. And thus America will at least be free to cope with its domestic problems and perhaps move a few steps nearer to realizing the American dream. The Russians, no longer threatened by outside dangers, will be able to devote most of their energies to building Communism at home, which is, of course, what they have wanted all along. Thus at long last the cold war will be liquidated and the era of truly peaceful competition (and, to a certain extent, cooperation) ushered in.

It is a beautiful vision and to some it may seem almost

sacrilege to subject it to critical examination. Yet man does not live by vision alone and the question has to be asked whether, and to what extent, the vision corresponds to the harsh facts of international life—not just to the desires of some well-meaning people. The concept of multipolarity may serve as a starting point for an investigation of this kind. But one cannot really deal with a concept in isolation from the realities of world power, the current changes in the international system. It can be done only in the course of a general *tour d'horizon* for which no apology may be needed.

"Current changes in the international system"—I use the term "system" with the greatest reluctance; everyone would benefit if there were an embargo on its use. Far too often the concept is used as if it were not a theoretical abstraction at all but had an existence of its own quite independent of its components. Perhaps it is one of those peculiarities which make the American language or, to be precise, its sweeping use, so puzzling for foreigners; thus, almost any group of people in America becomes a "community" even if its members have precious little in common. But such abuse of the language is not altogether harmless, since politicians sometimes borrow the terminology of the political scientists (unless, of course, it is too abstruse) to enrich their vocabularies. And they, too, may come to believe in the end that there really exists a "system" when in fact there is mainly confusion and anarchy.

It is difficult in retrospect to establish who invented the concept "multi-polar system"; it may have come up first in the debate on proliferation of nuclear weapons. But this question is not really of paramount importance; by now, at any rate, the concept has prevailed. President Nixon, in his report to Congress last February, announced the end of the bipolar postwar world "which opens to this generation a unique opportunity to create a new and lasting structure of peace." He also pointed to the "increasing self-reliance of the states created by the dissolution of empires and the growth of both their ability and determination to see to their own security and wellbeing."

A distinguished historian recently told us that it is a good thing that we have Russia as well as America (or America as well as Russia), "better still if we can have three such giants or four or five, better again, even to have seven."[10] The International Institute of Strategic Studies in its last yearly report announced the emergence of a new "great-power quadrilateral," a "genuinely global system with two non-white countries (China and Japan) firmly among the leaders. An American author has coined the term "Pentagonal World" and he did not mean the object of Norman Mailer's protest "march." In fairness it should be added that not every protagonist of multipolarity has regarded it as a panacea to all the world's ills. Stanley Hoffmann, to name but one, wrote in 1968 that not every multipolar system of the past has been moderate; "it is all too easy to imagine a multihierarchical system of dizzying instability."

But quite apart from the question of whether multipolarity makes for a more peaceful world, can it really be taken for granted that the concept corresponds to realities? That China and the Soviet Union are involved in a serious conflict is hardly a discovery of recent date; but neither the divisions in the Third World nor the lack of cohesion in the West necessarily make for the emergence of new centers of power. Politicians have to be optimists in their public statements and the phrases about "new and lasting structures of peace" come easily to them. Those who do not labor under such constraints will find less ground for optimism. What evidence is there of the ability and determination of the new countries to see to their own security and well-being? Or do the phrases simply mean that one assumes that most of these countries will somehow muddle through: that there will be no moment of truth in the years to come which would reveal their political impotence and inability (and perhaps also lack of determination) to take care of their security?

As far as the present-day world and the next decade are concerned, the emergence of new centers of power seems largely a chimera. There exist two-and-a-half major powers, with the rest of the world in a varying state of disarray. In the following, I shall first deal with the economic strength and the military power of the United States and the Soviet Union and the perspectives for the seventies.

The Economic Balance

Economic developments are in many ways the easiest to measure and compare. One need not be a Leninist to appreciate the importance of economic power. For more than four decades the Soviet leaders have promised to catch up with America and to overtake it. They have pointed with satisfaction and pride to the economic progress achieved by their system as compared with the stagnant, crisis-ridden capitalist world.

When the official program of the Communist Party of the Soviet Union was reformulated under Khrushchev, it stated unambiguously that "in the current decade (1961-1970) the Soviet Union will surpass the strongest and richest capitalist country, the United States, in production per head of population." Nineteen seventy has come and gone and this slogan has been replaced by a more modest one. According to the most recent announcements emanating from Moscow, the Soviet Union will surpass the present level of United States industrial and agricultural production in 1975. This, it is said, will be a "major milestone in the Soviet Union's economic competition with the capitalist countries." It is not an unrealistic prediction.

In 1971 more steel was produced in the Soviet Union than in the United States. As far as the production of coal is concerned, the Soviet Union overtook the United States as far back as 1958, and in cement in 1967. The Soviet Union also produces more pig iron and iron ore than the United States, and it is fairly certain that by 1975 the Soviet Union will produce more agricultural machinery as well as certain industrial and agricultural consumer goods than the United States. The Soviet G.N.P. was no more than one-third of the American in 1950; today it is about one-half.[11] Present Soviet plans in industry envisage a yearly growth of 8-9 percent, and it is expected that agricultural production in 1975 will be 20 percent or more above the current level. These are impressive figures and the Soviet leaders do not fail to recall that, owing to its superior social system, the Soviet Union has become the world's second economic power within a few decades—and that it expects to be first in the near future.

This is one side of the picture, but there are other aspects less encouraging from the Soviet point of view. I shall mention only some of them. 1) If the Soviet Union has made up ground in relative terms vis-à-vis the United States, the absolute distance is bigger than ever before, and it is likely to increase even further at least for some time to come even if the Soviet rate of growth were to become twice that of the United States. (The American G.N.P.—in 1966 dollars—was $414 billion in 1950, the Soviet G.N.P. $140 billion. The difference was $274 billion that year. At present it is $500 billion or more.)

2) Preoccupied with its race against the United States, the Soviet Union has ignored the emergence of two other economic giants, namely Western Europe and Japan. Soviet experts have suddenly discovered with an apparent sense of shock that these two have also made progress: the industrial output of Japan and the European Six, which had been 35 percent of the American output in 1950, reached 88 percent twenty years later.[12] The combined industrial output of the European Ten and Japan was not only considerably larger than that of the whole Comecon but also greater than that of the United States. If Russia produced more steel than the United States in 1971, Western European steel production was even more substantial. Even so, the growth rate of the Japanese steel industry, from 5 million tons in 1950 to 93 million in 1970, was far in excess of the Soviet. If Japan overtakes the Soviet Union in total industrial output in the near future, as some observers have predicted, this would constitute a serious ideological problem for Soviet leaders. Since fast growth rates have always been quoted by Communist leaders as proof of the superiority of the Soviet over the capitalist system, what then is the ideological lesson of the Japanese (and, to a lesser extent, of the West European) "miracle"?

3) Being preoccupied with "traditional" (i.e., partly outdated) industries, Soviet planners have only recently begun to pay due attention to the modern, science-oriented industries (electronics, computers, automation, chemical industry). They are much behind the West in this respect and there is little chance of their catching up with the United States or Japan in the near future.

4) Soviet hopes rest on Western countries' doing less well than in the sixties and on the assumption that the Soviet Union and its Comecon allies will fulfill, or exceed, the fairly high rates of

will fulfill, or exceed, the fairly high rates of growth upon which growth upon which they have decided. But neither supposition can be taken for granted without reservations. American real growth runs at present at 6 percent after two years of stagnation. Japanese growth has been down to an unprecedented low, 4.3 percent in 1971/72, but is again picking up momentum and may well be in excess of 7 percent in 1972/73. Several West European countries (including Germany and Italy) will certainly not do as well as in the sixties but will still make progress. The Soviet record on the other hand has been checkered in recent years: 1969 was fairly disastrous by Soviet standards (a growth rate of 2.3 percent), 1970 was excellent (8.5 percent), but 1971 was not outstanding (6 percent), partly as a result of a bad harvest. Soviet economists expect that the new protectionism in the West will result in a falling growth rate, stagnation and perhaps decline and political crisis. It is not certain that they will be right.

The Growth of G.N.P. in real terms.

	1970	1971	1972
W. Germany	5.5	2.8	2.0
France	6.0	5.4	5.0
Italy	5.0	0.9	3.5
Britain	2.1	1.0	3.5
U.S.A.	0.6	3.0	5.0
Japan	11.0	5.5	6.5
D.D.R.	5.5	4.5	5.0
U.S.S.R.	8.5	6.0	7.0

(The figures for 1971 are approximate, those for 1972 estimates.)

But there are also factors, albeit of a different character, inhibiting growth of the Soviet economy. Soviet resources in manpower are limited; as a result Soviet progress will depend on a very high, almost unprecedented, increase in productivity (36-40 percent for the Ninth Five-Year Plan). This, in turn, will depend to a large extent on the modernization of Soviet industry and the success of Soviet non-military R & D during the years to come.

In this respect, Soviet achievement has not been all that impressive. According to a report by Academic Kapitsa to the Academy of Sciences several years ago, the Soviet Union, with approximately the same number of scientific workers, produced only half as much scientific work as the Americans. Academician Sakharov and some colleagues, in a memorandum to the Soviet leadership, have stated that "we are ahead of the U.S. in the production of coal, but behind in the production of oil, gas and electric power, ten times behind in chemistry and immeasurably behind in computer technology. We are simply living in a different era." To make up this lag the Soviet leaders are eager to get the benefit of Western technology which is probably one of the main reasons behind the current wish for détente. But the problem will not be so easy to solve.

The Soviet Union will also have to do more for her consumers in the years to come, subsidizing agricultural prices and improving retail distribution. The Soviet consumer has so far enjoyed the fruits of economic expansion only to a relatively small extent. In the Soviet budget, private consumption has gone down as defense spending has gone up. Nominally, the Soviet per capita income is equal to that of Italy or Japan, but every tourist with unimpaired vision will realize within five minutes that standards are in fact considerably lower.

If present economic trends continue, there is every reason to assume that Japan, the Soviet Union, and Western Europe will make quicker progress than the United States for another few years. But what beyond this? If the scientists are right, a new technological revolution will totally change the world scene within the next ten to twenty years. (This refers to super conductivity, supersonic transport, weather control, control of thermonuclear energy resulting in the establishment of giant generating stations, the effects on industry of third generation computers, etc.) While America has been falling behind in the traditional industries such as textiles and steel production, its lead in the field of computers and electronics has been steadily increasing.

Since application of the new technology is very costly indeed, it has been predicted that it is not certain whether the Soviet Union and Japan will be able to keep up and that Western Europe will probably fall behind, unable to compete on the world markets. As a result Western Europe will suffer unemployment, a decline in efficiency and living standards, while politically and militarily being reduced to third class status. For, as the countries of Western Europe have been unable to pool and coordinate their efforts, they will no longer be capable of utilizing modern technology for military and civilian use. To a certain extent this is already the case, and unless the Europeans draw the obvious conclusions their position in the late seventies could become progressively more difficult.

These projections have to be taken seriously, even though some futurologists, carried away by their enthusiasm, have already come to regard civilian technology as the one vital aspect in world affairs in the years to come. This, of course, is not the case, if only because political factors, both domestic and international, may well inhibit (or hasten) the new technological revolution. A highly advanced technology is a prerequisite for political power but is not by itself power. In fact, it may be perfectly compatible, in certain circumstances, with political impotence.

Such discussions will be anathema to the growing number of critics of unrestricted ("exponential") economic growth who have been alarmed by pollution, adverse changes in climate, the growing scarcity of mineral and other resources, the danger of starvation and, above all, the inability so far of bringing population growth under control. But in this field as in so many others, there simply is no meeting of minds between West and East. While the West debates the pros and cons of zero economic growth, the Communist powers' supreme aim remains maximum growth:

> While the U.S. debates the possible ecological hazards of the Alaskan pipeline, the Soviet Union published boasts of the "world's longest gas pipeline." While American nuclear power stations are being stalled by protests, the Soviet Union is building reactors with a capacity of a million kilowatts or more, and is planning many more. While a wave of anti-technology sentiment in the U.S. killed the supersonic transport project and reduced spending for basic research and space explorations, the Soviet Union is apparently expanding its support in such fields on the

ground that science and technology are indispensible foundations of growth and progress. . . .[13]

It is not difficult to understand the Soviet and Chinese attitude: since they lag behind the advanced capitalist countries, an economic slow-down would perpetuate their inferiority. One day, having drawn level and overtaken the non-Communist world, they may well opt for deceleration. Having advocated unrestricted population growth for a long time they have, after all, retreated in practice, if not always in theory, from the dogma of anti-Malthusianism. But so far as industrial growth is concerned, a retreat from current policies is almost unthinkable in the near future. These policies are deeply anchored in Communist theory and practice, and radical change in this respect, though perhaps inevitable in the long run, will be a difficult and protracted process.

The present survey deals with the prospects for the seventies. As far as this period is concerned, it can be predicted with reasonable certainty that, despite a slowing down of economic expansion in the West and in Japan, the economic balance of power is not going to change radically. "Looking ahead a decade—who is so foolish as to look further?—we are right to neglect economics."[14]

The Military Balance

The essential facts about the military balance are not really in dispute.[15] Their interpretations, however, diverge widely. The dispute is not easy to understand for non-specialists who may have heard of SHAPE and ICBM but will not know the difference between a SLBM and an SRBM, let along between AWX and FOXBAT. Mathematical theorizing about arms races of the "interactive determinism" school or "probabilistic strategic modeling" will only further confuse them and it is doubtful whether the effort to understand the theories is worthwhile since they are largely based on unreal assumptions.

Over and above the linguistic difficulties, there is a tendency among many of our students of strategy to comment on strategic issues as if they were a subject divorced from politics. When they do bring in politics, they are mainly influenced in their thinking by domestic considerations. The assessment of the other side's capacities and intentions of some students of defense policies is colored, and sometimes distorted, by what they think of the present administration. They may or may not be right in assuming that successive American presidents and administrations have done a bad job. They may or may not be correct in maintaining that America cannot afford a big defense budget. But to make their point more effectively, they frequently play down the other side's strength and describe its aims as more innocuous than they really are.

Three schools of thought exist, broadly speaking, and the SALT agreement has hardly affected their arguments. The first maintains that, as a result of the massive Soviet military buildup since the middle sixties, an imbalance has come into being which will grow during the years to come and reduce the United States to second-class power status unless a major attempt is made now to check this dangerous trend. While the United States has settled for parity (or "sufficiency"), the Soviet Union has built up its forces beyond the level needed for deterrence and seems to aim in the long run at superiority. Quantitatively the United States is now inferior to the Soviet Union; if as a result of further defense cuts America should lose its technological lead, an American president may have to crawl (to use Secretary Laird's phrase) to any negotiating table anywhere in the world. "The road to peace has never been through appeasement, unilateral disarmament or negotiation from weakness ... Weakness of the U.S. of its military capability and its will—would be the gravest threat to the peace of the world."[16] True, the SALT agreement has put a ceiling on the production of certain arms, but the qualitative arms race will continue, the effort to increase the power and the accuracy of existing weapons will continue with undiminished vigor. Or, to be precise, the United States will be at a great disadvantage, for, in the conditions of false peace, euphoria, and pseudo-détente, American defense planners will find it much more difficult than the Russians to get the allocations they need to keep peace with the other side.

The second school of thought regards this appraisal as far too alarmist. True, the Soviet Union has caught up with the United States and in some respects overtaken it; it has more than 1600 ICBMs as against 1054 American missiles, a more modern fleet, and will probably overtake the United States in the construction of Polaris-type submarines this year or next. The political implications, however, should not be overdramatized since the Soviet Union reached "rough parity" anyway ten years ago. Furthermore the Soviets, too, face considerable constraints (economic rather than political) and as the nuclear treaty shows, have realized that any attempt to attain a first-strike capacity would be ruinously expensive, quite apart from the fact that in all probability it would be doomed to failure. Seen from this vantage point the present Soviet buildup has been a futile exercise in "overkill," it does not really affect the strategic balance. Uri Ra'anan has recently summarized the views of this group in the following way: "As they see it, there is an adversary relationship not so much between the U.S. and the U.S.S.R. as between both and a third—almost personalized—element, namely the Arms Spiral." The latter is thought to have an organic life of its own, somehow independent of the political contest between the powers. Both Washington and Moscow are believed to be in its thrall, mechanically playing their prescribed roles in a mutually damaging, continually escalating version of the "action-reaction dialogue." It was this syndrome, "which made the Soviet Union resort to this superfluous accelerated armaments program, because the U.S. for some years kept widening the missile gap in its favor to the point where the U.S.S.R. felt impelled to react. They feel reassured, however, that the Soviet Union remains far short of a genuine first-strike capability . . ."[17]

The third school of thought maintains that spokesmen for defense constitute a lobby whose statements cannot, *a priori,* be given any credence. They have always exaggerated Soviet military power (Kennedy's famous "missile gap" which never was) in order to get more money out of Congress. For years, American military spokesmen have predicted that the Russians would soon have MIRVs (multiple independently targetable reentry vehicles). But the Russians have in fact lagged behind in this respect, and as a result the gap in missile warheads is widening rapidly in favor of the United States. This imbalance would have grown sharply in the years to come. Realizing this, the Russians feared that "we are trying for some kind of counter-force, preemptive or first-strike capacity."[18] As for the Soviet Navy—it is really not very dangerous because, according to Mr. Stone "it has no warm weather (sic—read "water") ports." Anyway the cold war is over, military power is no longer an instrument of political power in the present-day world and, for that reason, the arms race is quite pointless. If Soviet military leaders have nevertheless continued to talk about "victory" in a future war, it is merely a reflection of "insecurity and inferiority:" once again the United States has succeeded in frightening the leaders of the Soviet Union.[19] Now that agreement has been reached on the limitation of strategic arms, it should be followed up by a drastic reduction of the arms budget, unilateral, if necessary.

* * * * *

What should one make of these conflicting interpretations? The first school of thought correctly stresses the dangers facing the United States—not today but in a few years hence if it does not keep up its guard. American technological superiority in the military field is not that substantial; if American spending on defense R & D should fall much below the Soviet level, the result would be more or less predictable. Nevertheless, arguments of the second and third schools also contain grains of truth—though not with regard to Soviet aims and intentions. These they interpret on the whole by applying American standards of political behavior. But they *are* right to the extent that, as of now and for a number of years to come, American power is such that it would not greatly matter if the Russians achieved numerical superiority in one specific field or another.

It is also true that military spokesmen tend to assume the worst and that they exaggerate potential dangers to obtain budgetary allocations. They would be derelict in their duties if they acted differently, just as a physician or a lawyer could not be trusted if, in a diagnosis, he ruled out the worst. It is quite true that such an approach has its dangers not only with regard to overspending. By emphasizing Soviet strength and Western weakness, American military spokesmen move on slippery ground: the adverse political effect may sometimes outweigh the military gain. By painting a black picture of America's defense capacity, the Pentagon may get the money it needs for new bombers and nuclear submarines. But at the same time America's European and Far Eastern allies may reach the conclusion that, if American strength has declined so much, its commitments can no longer be relied upon. This is one of several handicaps facing Western defense planners in contrast to their colleagues in the Soviet bloc. Nevertheless, it seems fairly certain that, unless American defense spending falls substantially below the Soviet level, the strategic balance is unlikely to change radically during the next few years and, as in economics, it is impossible to make any predictions beyond that date.

With all this there is, of course, a basic imbalance between the United States and the Soviet Union quite irrespective of statistics on defense spending, missiles, and nuclear submarines. For, given the fact that the Soviet strategic force neutralizes American power, other factors will be of decisive importance; credibility, the perception of power and the ability and readiness to exercise it. Power, like justice, has to be seen to exist.

In this respect the situation could hardly be more different. The image of America as far as the outside world is concerned has more and more become that of a country wishing to reduce its outside commitments, a nation beset by defeatism, ridden by internal dissent. On the other hand there is the Soviet Union, purposeful, dynamic, out to win the global struggle rather than to preserve the status quo. There are no guilt feelings in the Soviet Union about being powerful; on the contrary, there is widespread belief—at least among the leadership—that other countries too should be made to share the blessings of a system which has made Russia so powerful.

There is a great and still growing self-confidence in the Soviet Union; as America retreats from "globalism" and "intervention-ism" there is bound to be a shift in favor of the Soviet Union in the overall balance of power. It will be said that this description grossly overstates American weaknesses and exaggerates Soviet strength. But the semblance of power counts as much as its reality in Europe, in the Third World, and, of course, in the Soviet Union. The political consequences could be serious and far-reaching.

Such fears, needless to say, refer to the years to come. The belief that the American ship is sinking is not yet widespread in Europe or Japan, and the Russians still have a healthy respect for American power. It could further be argued that, if the Russians indeed believe that the tide is turning in their favor, they will not want to risk their gain by unnecessary head-on confrontations. But there is yet another aspect favoring the Soviet Union. Other things being equal, it will be conventional forces and local balances of power that will count in future local conflicts; fortunately there is no good reason to expect any other kind of conflict. In most potential danger zones, the Soviet Union posesses the advantages of geographical proximity and initiative. Moscow can put the heat on and off at will—be it in Europe, the Middle East, or Southeast Asia. It may decide not to make use of its advantages, perhaps on the assumption that the next decade will see further weakening of American power, disunity in Europe and perhaps disintegration in China, all of which would make an aggressive Soviet foreign policy unnecessary and indeed contra-indicated.

To summarize: The relation in strength between the United States and the Soviet Union has not decisively changed in recent years in either the economic or the military field, and a major reversal in this respect seems unlikely at the present time. There have been, however, political and psychological changes which may affect the balance of power. As for the emergence of new superpowers; on closer inspection they are found lacking in those attributes that in the final analysis are essential to a superpower.

New League of Superpowers

Of the members of the "new league of superpowers" none have been the subject of more extravagant claims than Japan:

"Japan's emergence to its new post-war status is the result of its gradual though impressive evolution to the rank of the third powerful economic country in the world in the 1970s" writes Andrew J. Pierre. He continues, "Although Japan's strength today is primarily measurable in economic terms, history teaches us that such strength is sooner or later translated into political and military power."[20]

Whether history teaches us anything of the sort is questionable. One could think of a great many economic giants in the past that were not exactly powerful politically—or that were defeated by countries much inferior to them economically. Genghis Khan, on the other hand, was not among the leading steel producers of his period. But even if history did teach us a clear lesson, it is more than doubtful whether it would be applicable in a new and, in some essential respects, unique historical situation.

According to Herman Kahn, Japan is bound to emerge within the next two decades as an economic and technological superstate. According to Hisao Kanamori, of the Japanese Economic Planning Agency, per capita income in Japan in the early eighties will be level with that of the United States and almost three times as high as that of Britain.[21] In other words (and putting it more dramatically) Japan's economy will have overtaken America's (whose population is twice as large) around 1990. It will have outdistanced the Soviet Union well before that—perhaps even in the present decade. European experts concurred: according to the International Institute of Strategic Studies' yearly report, Japan began emerging in 1971 together with China, ready to join the Soviet Union and the United States in a new world-wide concert of major power. Both Mr. Kanamori and Mr. Kahn, and some other observers as well, assume that Japan will have the technological momentum, the work force (as well as the work ethos), and the export markets to make such growth possible, if not inevitable. Labor shortages, inflation, environmental problems, possible changes in world trade patterns (they base their calculations on a yearly world-trade expansion of about 10 percent) were thought to be of limited importance.

Less than a year has passed and the euphoria has given way to much more sober assessments. It has been realized that an economy so much oriented toward exports is unbalanced and hence vulnerable, that Japanese exports will face difficulties in the future in the United States and Europe, and that there are limits to what the Far Eastern market will be able to buy from Japan. To give but one example: Thailand's trade deficit with Japan already exceeds that country's total foreign exchange reserves. Some of the present difficulties are probably transient in character, but others are structural and may well inhibit economic growth in the years to come.

For Japan 1971 was a year of multiple shocks. While some foreign commentators predicted that the twenty-first century would be Japan's, the mood inside Japan has been far more subdued. Japanese policy makers have asked themselves whether they should look for a détente with Russia or China, or perhaps both, and how these aims could be combined; whether they should opt for unarmed neutrality, whether Japan's viability as a nation could, or could not, be ensured without maintaining a close link with the United States. There is a great deal of heart searching in Japan but none of the confidence befitting a superpower.

The Chinese maintain that the present crisis is bound to propel Japan toward militarization. They point to the fact that, despite the 1947 constitution (which banned the maintenance of military forces), self-defense units are established and equipped not only with rifles but also with tanks, missiles, submarines, destroyers, and a thousand planes. Between 1972 and 1976 about $16 billion will be spent for extending and improving the Japanese army. As a result, Japan will move from twelfth to seventh place as far as defense spending is concerned. According to some experts, Japan will be able to produce Minuteman-type missiles within three years. If Japan should decide to produce nuclear devices and missiles she will have been influenced, above all, by the Chinese example which has shown the way to gain international recognition as a world power, a permanent seat on the Security Council, and other such fringe benefits.

Such assessments ignore, however, both the general context of Far Eastern politics and the strong forces opposing Japanese remilitarization. In 1970 Japan spent less than 0.8 percent of its G.N.P. on defense, the lowest by far of any country of comparable size and population. (Under the Fourth Defense Buildup program this will go up to 1 percent.) Influential circles on both the left and the right favor a revision of the security pact with the United States, or its abolition. But remilitarization is not at all easy under present circumstances both in view of Japan's pacifist constitution and in view of internal opposition. Paragraph 9 of the constitution, which prohibits offensive weapons, a conscription system, and sending troops overseas, can be reinterpreted (or sidestepped) to a certain extent, but antimilitarist popular feeling is a very different proposition.

Japanese foreign policy took the American nuclear umbrella for granted during the last twenty-five years. Now there are doubts whether America will be able and willing to honor its commitments even if the Seventh Fleet remains and if air force units continue to be stationed as before in the Philippines, Guam and Okinawa. Statements made in Washington about the end of bipolarism have produced declarations in Tokyo about the age of multipolarization and the need for a foreign policy "divorced from ideology." But being a major exporter does not make Japan a major power center and the number of options open to it are very limited indeed. A neutralist policy would probably best correspond to moods prevailing in Tokyo. But neutralism plus rearmament would provoke even greater Chinese hostility than a Japanese-American alliance. The Japanese could sign a non-aggression pact with the Soviet Union any day but this would be a meaningless gesture. An attempt to improve relations with China would be more significant, but the Russians would hardly like it; in view of China's distrust of Japan it would take a great effort to normalize relations between the two countries.

Japan is now the world's greatest consumer of raw materials, but most of them are shipped from thousands of miles away; obviously remilitarization would not solve this problem. The Japanese economy has invested great efforts to boost its trade with China. In 1971 this trade reached an all time high, but still amounts to less than a billion dollars. There will no more be an "explosion" in Japanese-Chinese than in American-Soviet trade.

China's foreign trade today is in fact hardly bigger than in the 1920s and there is no good reason to assume that it will greatly increase; the myth of unlimited possibilities of the Chinese market dies hard. The Soviet Union would be only too eager to increase its trade with Japan, but it insists, as in its dealings with the West, on low interest loans offering payment in oil over a period of twenty years starting in 1978. Such conditions, needless to say, are not very attractive from the Japanese point of view.

This leaves, as before, the United States and Europe as Japan's leading customers by a wide margin. The United States has absorbed over 30 percent of Japan's exports in recent years and Japan is America's second best customer after Canada (15 percent in 1970). The essential facts about Japan's positive balance of payment are known: the Japanese claim that up to 1965 their payment balance with the United States was negative and that Japan's gain at present is relatively small (some $400 million); the "Japanese invasion," in other words, is largely a myth. The American argument is, very briefly, that Japan has refused to liberalize its trade, that it buys from America mainly raw materials and exports highly sophisticated machinery—which it refuses to buy from America. Japan's trade with Western Europe is smaller. It has greatly increased during the last year, but problems facing Japan in Europe are very similar in the long run: Japan has been selling ships, cars, and electronic equipment; it has bought from Europe whisky, expensive woolens, and confectioneries. This has resulted in measures limiting Japanese imports to Europe. The Japanese now realize the necessity of having a larger measure of reciprocity and "voluntary self-control" but, given the limited size of the Japanese domestic market and the structure of Japanese industry, this is easier said than done.

There will be no easy way out of the dilemma. Economic growth in all probability will not continue on the past phenomenal level. Social conflicts may become more intense and there are signs of growing polarization on the domestic front. Japan is a striking example of the fact that G.N.P. is not a synonym for power. Japanese leaders have complained that they have been cold-shouldered by the Americans despite the fact that they have the greatest power potential in the Far East. But the

Soviet attitude has been similar. China's G.N.P. is less than half of Japan's, yet the Russians are very seriously worried about China and do not lose a minute's sleep over Japan. These, then, are the realities of power in 1972.

For Japan the postwar era ended with the *dollar shoku* and President Nixon's visit to Peking. She does not want to remain (to quote a Tokyo correspondent) quietly on the sidelines but wishes to explore a new role in the new multipolar system. Like Western Europe, she will, alas, go on exploring for a long time.

Today's Europe

The two encouraging features characterizing contemporary Europe are (relative) prosperity and peace; there has been no war in Europe and there is no reason to assume that there will be one. Considering the state of Europe at the end of the Second World War, the economic and cultural revival of the Continent is almost a miracle. I see no reason to revise what I wrote on another occasion, summarizing a quarter of a century of European history since 1945: "Far from 'dying in convulsions' as Sartre had predicted, Europe has shown a new vigour which has astonished friend and foes alike."[22] But Europe is not one of the five pillars of a new "pentagonal world system;" in fact, the very notion of Europe as a center of power is so incongruous, considering the present state of affairs, that the necessity of seriously discussing such a contention is not readily obvious.

The internal situation in many European countries is, to put it mildly, far from stable. The political climate in Britain has deteriorated during the last year both as a result of the situation in Ulster and social tensions. The internal consensus on basic issues, or to be precise, the underlying assumption that political struggle ought to be carried out in accordance with certain generally accepted rules no longer exists. There is a lack of responsibility and indeed a silliness in British politics, such as that reflected, for instance, in the Labor party's official attitude toward European unity for which there is almost no precedent in recent British history. The Irish, curiously enough, have been much more farsighted in this respect. The danger that France will revert to the bad old days of the Fourth Republic is by no means over; the internal malaise which manifested itself in 1968 still exists. Pompidou and his government have shown little ability for real leadership, and have been discredited by several embarrassing *affaires.* The less said about the Italian and Turkish domestic scenes, the better.

In Germany, too, the political climate has become uglier and the polarization between opposing forces much sharper. The German universities still exist: lectures are still given, professors still draw their salaries and students still graduate. But standards in what were once the world's greatest institutions of higher learning have fallen to an alarming extent during the last few years as a result of the prevailing political climate. In Chancellor Brandt's party the influence of a new generation is increasingly felt and is showing purpose and tactical ability. But in their ideological inspiration they are closer to the Communist party than to Social Democracy. If they take over the party, or cause its defeat in the next election, the result may well be disastrous for Germany.

Franco's reign nears its inglorious end and the Greek colonels will not last forever; it is difficult to imagine that the transition to democracy will be peaceful—if there is to be such a transition, which is by no means certain. It is ironic that these two dictatorships are among the European countries which have made the most economic progress but this is, as long experience shows, no guarantee of stability. Sweden and to a lesser extent Norway and Denmark is affected by deep internal discontent, and even in the Benelux countries domestic crises have been more frequent and protracted. There are signs of disintegration in Yugoslavia, which belongs to neither West nor East, and the question of what will happen once Tito disappears from the political scene troubles both the Yugoslavs and their neighbors.

Optimists will argue that such crises are part of the normal democratic process; that in living memory Europe has never been free of tensions of this kind; that the Labor Party will ultimately say "yes" to Europe; that Italy will somehow muddle through; that Brandt, Heath, and Pompidou realize the necessity for closer European collaboration and that, given time and Russia's preoccupation with China, there is no serious danger that Europe will fall apart. This may be so, but Europe lives on borrowed time. For reasons already indicated, closer European economic cooperation now—not ten years hence—is imperative. The Continent's present economic strength is deceptive and unless it pools its resources it will stagnate and fall behind.

There is no common European foreign and defense policy. Europe has instead shown an inertia, and in some cases a shortsightedness and paralysis of will, which is bound to inspire observers with deep pessimism. Senator Mansfield's complaints are in part only too justified: Why should 250 million Europeans, with great industrial resources and long military experience, be unable to organize an effective military coalition to defend themselves? There is nothing basically wrong with Brandt's *Ostpolitik;* the agreements with Russia and Poland should have been signed long ago. In some ways the *Ostpolitik* does not even go far enough; since recognition of the D.D.R. is inevitable anyway, it might as well be granted now. Danger comes not from the *Ostpolitik* itself but from the illusions engendered by it, even by Brandt himself and some of his colleagues who have talked on various occasions about a historical turning point in Europe and have predicted a radical improvement in West-East relations.

Ostpolitik, needless to say, is the long-delayed official recognition of the fact that Germany lost the war, but there is no reason to assume that it will bring about a "real détente." It should be made a rule, as the *Economist* recently commented, that such words as "détente," "cold war" and "relaxation of tensions" be outlawed from the discussion. For these are fog-making words which encourage people to think that tensions have existences of their own, separate from the conflict of interests that gives rise to the tensions. Pompidou and his ministers are all in favor of closer cooperation and are afraid that American troops will be withdrawn from Europe. But at the same time they want others to pay the price of European unity; the protection of inefficient French agriculture is still a far more important consideration as far as they are concerned.

The defense policy of the Scandinavian countries has more in common with "Alice in Wonderland" than with harsh European realities. Sweden still earnestly insists on neutrality, though it has virtually given up attempting to make its neutrality credible, as it did during the Second World War and the years after. Iceland's only contribution to Nato has been the American base at Keflavik which it now wants removed. Denmark spends little more than 2 percent of its G.N.P. on defense and the ruling Social Democrats want further drastic reductions. General Walker, the former (British) Nato Commander North stated only the obvious when he said that such a scheme would make it impossible to get allied assistance to Denmark in case of war, and that, generally speaking, Scandinavia could not be defended if the governments concerned were not willing to make a greater effort.

These neutralist leanings would make sense if there were no political pressure and no military threat. But the Scandinavian countries are in fact under constant pressure from the Soviet Union, reflected, for instance, in Sweden's almost pathetic efforts not to give offense to Russia. The Soviet Union has established in the Murmansk-Kola region what the Norwegian minister of defense has called "the world's mightiest complex of bases," and Warsaw Pact superiority in the Baltic Sea is 5 to 1 and still growing. The Soviet Union has a most impressive naval task force standing by throughout the year between the coast of Norway and the North of Scotland—neither for fishing nor, in view of the inclement weather, for reasons of health.

The "Scandinavian syndrome" is reflected in Western Europe's attitude to the Soviet proposal for a European (security) conference. If the Soviet intention was détente—the reduction of armaments, the inviolability of existing borders, collective security, the repudiation of the threat or use of force, the promotion of trade and so on—no sane person in West Europe would be entitled to object. The Russians have treaties with France and Germany providing for these praiseworthy aims and they could have similar agreements within a number of days with every other European country. But Soviet intentions are a little more ambitious; they do not just want to transform, as they maintain, relations between European states "to help overcome the division of the continent into military-political groupings." On the contrary, they want to strengthen the cohesion of the

Warsaw Pact countries while keeping Western Europe disunited. They argue that the Communist countries constitute a "natural" bloc, tied together by ideological, economic and other ties. But they claim that, since the non-Communist countries of Europe have no such common interests, their unity is "artificial." The overriding long term aim of a European conference as far as the Russians are concerned is not just collective security but a lasting peace—*Pax Sovietica.* They do not for a moment contemplate the dissolution of the Warsaw Pact; rightly so, from their point of view, for it would result within a very short time in the disintegration of their bloc.[23]

The Soviet Union maintains that it wants to expand its trade with Western Europe, and many Western businessmen would be only too eager to reciprocate. Yet the statistics show that Soviet trade with Germany was relatively less in 1971 (1.3 percent!) than ten years earlier. Trade between Comecon and the E.E.C., which was about 12 percent in the sixties, is now declining to about 7-9 percent. There are no "artificial barriers" any longer. The real reason for this decline is that Comecon has no convertible currency. Moreover, the Russians decided several years ago that, within the framework of their twenty-year integration program, most of the trade of the Comecon countries should be with each other rather than with the West. The Russians want long-term loans from West Europe to finance imports and the Europeans have been quite helpful in this respect; but Europe's financial resources are not unlimited. In brief, it is doubtful whether even in the economic field a European conference would serve a useful purpose.

The whole concept of a European conference has been befogged to such an extent by empty and misleading slogans that it is questionable whether it would be the right forum in which to discuss concrete problems with the Russians such as the balanced reduction of armed forces on which there is a common interest. The objection to the European conference (to quote the *Economist* again) is that at best it would be a bore, a sort of mini-United Nations assembly in which tired politicians exchange tireder platitudes. At worst it could be something more dangerous. Yet such is the general aimlessness of Western

European politics that such a conference now seems quite likely; for all one knows it may become a permanent institution. The whole affair may be of no consequence in the long run. But it shows better than any other illustration the weakness of Western Europe, its inability to take the initiative, to assert its interests, or to shape a common policy. The problem facing Western Europe, in brief, is one of survival, of how to maintain security and independence in the face of gradual American retreat from "globalism." The idea that Western Europe will be able to play a major part in the new concert of powers is about as realistic as the assumption that a one-legged man could win the high jump in the Olympics.

China and Asia

China, in contrast to Japan and Western Europe, is a factor of major importance in the new "international system," not so much as a global power but certainly as one within the Asian framework. Its example again shows that economic performance does not count for that much. For a fairly long time the world has been treated to accounts of the marvelous work done by Chinese workers and peasants, the wise and farsighted policy of their leaders, the incredible achievements of their barefooted scientists. These claims are by now wearing a little thin. Mao and his colleagues have been in power for almost a quarter of a century, yet economically China is still a very backward country. Her pride is steel production—21 million tons in 1971 (incidentally, one of the few figures published)—but the capacity to produce 22 million tons already existed ten years ago. China's grain harvest in 1971 was 245 million tons, which was less than in 1958, despite the fact that her population has grown by many millions since. Electricity and oil production (about 25 million tons) is small by any standard and will limit the scope of economic expansion during coming years. With a per capita income of about $145, China is still among the poorest countries in the world.

Unlike Japan and Western Europe, however, China has given absolute priority to defense. She carried out her first atomic test in October 1964, her first full-scale thermonuclear test in June 1967. The transition time between these two was less than three years; the French needed eight. In April 1970, the Chinese launched their first satellite with a payload weighing twice as much as Sputnik 1. They began to build ICBMs in 1965; though progress was not as fast as expected. Nevertheless they were able to deploy early in 1972 a handful of new missiles with a range of up to 2,500 miles, which means that Moscow is now in the reach of Chinese missiles.

It is not known whether a preemptive nuclear strike has ever been seriously considered in Moscow. But there is no doubt that the Chinese threat figures very prominently in Soviet thought; the number of Soviet divisions deployed along the Chinese borders is believed to be forty-four at present. The image of the Chinese enemy (in contrast to the American) is that of a tough and ruthless fighter, inflexible, who will not hesitate to use any devious strategem, any weapon to achieve his aim. Soviet leaders, however, seem to speculate on the lack of stability inside China. That Mao and his colleagues will be replaced by a pro-Soviet clique is probably beyond their wildest hopes. But is it that unlikely that the struggle for power between rival contenders—the tensions between army and party (and within the party and the army), the various centrifugal trends (China's twenty-eight regions pursue diverging politics in many respects)—will again paralyze China as it did during the Cultural Revolution? Such a process would not, of course, altogether remove the "Chinese danger" but it would greatly reduce it, while making it possible for the Soviet Union to pursue a more energetic foreign policy in other parts of the world. Peking's influence on the world Communist movement is likely to shrink as the national components in Chinese communism become more prominent; the appeal of Maoism outside China (and outside the Chinese diaspora) was always based to a certain extent on a misunderstanding. Nevertheless, whatever happens on the domestic scene, China will still be the most populous country on earth and its military strength cannot be ignored. It will figure prominently in the political calculations of Russia, Japan, and India. But it will not be a global power for a long time to come.

The American retreat from "globalism" unquestionably creates a new situation; the balance of power is changing—but not necessarily towards multipolarity. There is no symmetry between the two superpowers. While America is in retreat, the Soviet Union still has a global policy. While the United States has opted for disengagement, the Soviet Union increases its commitments. To this extent, irrespective of America's economic performance and strategic might, the Soviet Union is now in a superior position. It is unlikely that Mr. Brzezinski would still maintain—as he did not so long ago—that "the U.S. is today the only effective global military power in the world." The assumption that Japan and Western Europe have emerged, or are about to emerge, as new global power centers is quite unwarranted. The shrinking of the American umbrella will compel Europe and Japan to fend for themselves. Whether they will succeed in weathering the coming storms is uncertain. A world power (let alone a "superpower") is capable of asserting its interests and aims beyond its borders. Yet Western Europe and Japan, with all their economic resources and potential, have no such capacity; as for their defense, they are more dependent on outside help than, say, Australia or Brazil. There is, in short, no multipolar system emerging, unless one accepts this as a euphemism for the spread of confusion, and possibly chaos. The American retreat is causing different sorts of power vacuums which may eventually be somehow filled. The assumption that this will result in a more peaceful and more democratic world makes sense only if coupled with a belief in the intervention of a supernatural force in the not-too-distant future. But then the supernatural force, too, may have been converted to non-interventionism.

NOTES

1. James A. Johnson, "The New Generation of Isolationists," *Foreign Affairs,* October 1970.
2. *Foreign Policy,* 5 (1971), p. 118.
3. M. Roskin: "What New Isolationism?", *Foreign Policy,* 6 1972.
4. Manfred Jonas: *Isolationism in America 1935-41.* Cornell University Press, 1966, *passim.*
5. "A Spheres of Influence Policy," *Foreign Policy,* 5 and 6, 1971/2.
6. Fulbright: *The Arrogance of Power,* pp. 78-80, 203, 215.
7. Stilman & Pfaff: *Power and Impotence,* pp. 77, 200.
   H. Morgenthau: *A New Foreign Policy for the U.S.,* New York, 1969, p. 55.
   R. Steel: *Pax Americana,* p. 323.
   G. Allison: "Cool It: The Foreign Policy of Young America," *Foreign Policy,* Winter 1970/71.
   D. Calleo: *The Atlantic Fantasy,* Baltimore, 1970, p. 81.
8. *Washington Post,* 28 May 1972, quoting *Foreign Policy,* Summer 1972.
9. Universe Books, New York, 1972.
10. Sir Herbert Butterfield: *The Discontinuities between the Generations in History* (The Rede lecture 1971) Cambridge, 1972.
11. Most of this advance was achieved in the 1950s; between 1960-69 the Soviet economy made virtually no progress improving its relative position vis-à-vis the United States.
12. "Three Centers of World Capitalism" (in Russian); *World Economics and International Relations,* March 1972, p. 97.
13. John Noble Wilford in a dispatch from Moscow. *New York Times,* March 30, 1972.
14. "Declining Self Confidence" Peter Wiles, *International Affairs* 1971.
15. This statement does not, admittedly, refer to the extent of Soviet defense spending. According to official Soviet statements it is 8%, and some Western commentators put it as high as 15.2% of the G.N.P. (M. Boretsky in "Economic Perform-

ance and the Military Burden in the Soviet Union," Washington 1970). This would imply that Soviet military funding equals that of the United States. Since the Soviet Union does not publish detailed figures about defense spending, and since no one in the West can know for certain how much a "defense ruble" is worth, the discussions among Western experts are likely to continue for a long time. (See Alec Nove: "Soviet Defence Spending" in *Survival,* October 1971 and Boretsky's rejoinder in the same journal.)

16. See for instance the reports of the Blue Ribbon Defense Plan published in July 1970 and in March 1971; also "The Military Unbalance" published by the National Strategy Information Center (New York, 1971) and W. Kintner and R. Pfaltzgraff: "Soviet Military Trends: Implications for U.S. Security" (Washington, 1971).

17. "The Changing American-Soviet Strategic Balance: Some Political Implications." Printed for the use of the Senate Committee on Government Operation, Washington, 1972.

18. I. F. Stone in *New York Review,* March 23, 1972.

19. Edgar M. Bottome: *The Balance of Terror,* Boston, 1972, p. 205.

20. "Europe and America in a Pentagonal World" in *Survey,* Winter 1972.

21. "Japan's Economy in 1985," Tokyo, April 1971.

22. *Europe since Hitler,* 1970.

23. Perhaps the Soviet leaders should have accepted the advice offered by Mr. Ronald Steel: "A communist Poland does not offer much more military safety for the Soviet Union than does a neutral Poland." (*Pax Americana,* 1967). But they have refused to accept such counsel—perhaps because they do not share Mr. Steel's basic assumptions such as "today there is no Soviet bloc." The Communist party of Czechoslovakia is equal in authority to the Communist party of the Soviet Union . . ." (*Ibid.*)